THE LUZUMIYAT OF ABU'L-ALA

ABU AL-ALA AL-MAARRI

Translated by
AMEEN FARES RIHANI

IV EDITIONS

CONTENTS

TO HIS ROYAL HIGHNESS
EMIR FEISAL
IN WHOM ARE CENTRED
THE HOPES AND ASPIRATIONS
OF THE SYRIAN PEOPLE
FOR A UNITED SYRIA
THIS BOOK
IS DEDICATED

THE LUZUMIYAT OF ABU'L-ALA

Selected from his
Luzum ma la Yalzam and Suct uz-Zand
and first rendered into English

By

AMEEN RIHANI

Author of
The Book of Khaled

TO ABU'L-ALA

In thy fountained peristyles of Reason
Glows the light and flame of desert noons;
And in the cloister of thy pensive Fancy
Wisdom burns the spikenard of her moons.

Closed by Fate the portals of the dwelling
Of thy sight, the light thus inward flowed;
And on the shoulders of the crouching Darkness
Thou hast risen to the highest road.

I have seen thee walking with Canopus
Through the stellar spaces of the night;
I have heard thee asking thy Companion,
"Where be now my staff, and where thy light?"

Abu'l-Ala, in the heaving darkness,
Didst thou not the whisperings hear of me?

In thy star-lit wilderness, my Brother,
Didst thou not a burdened shadow see?

I have walked and I have slept beside thee,
I have laughed and I have wept as well;
I have heard the voices of thy silence
Melting in thy Jannat and thy hell.

I remember, too, that once the Saki
Filled the antique cup and gave it thee;
Now, filled with the treasures of thy wisdom,
Thou dost pass that very cup to me.

By the God of thee, my Syrian Brother,
Which is best, the Saki's cup or thine?
Which the mystery divine uncovers—
If the cover covers aught divine.

And if it lies hid in the soul of silence
Like incense in the dust of ambergris,
Wouldst thou burn it to perfume the terror
Of the caverns of the dried-up seas?

Where'er it be, Oh! let it be, my Brother.—
Though "thrice-imprisoned,"9 thou hast forged
us more
Solid weapons for the life-long battle
Than all the Heaven-taught Armorers of yore.

"Thrice-imprisoned," thou wert e'en as mighty,

In the boundless kingdom of the mind,
As the whirlwind that compels the ocean,
As the thunder that compels the wind.

"Thrice-imprisoned," thou wert freer truly
Than the liegeless Arab on his mare,—
Freer than the bearers of the sceptre,—
Freer than the winged lords of the air.

"Thrice-imprisoned," thou hast sung of freedom
As but a few of all her heroes can;
Thou hast undermined the triple prison
Of the mind and heart and soul of man.

In thy fountained peristyles of Reason
Glows the light and flame of desert noons;
And in the cloister of thy pensive Fancy
Wisdom burns the spikenard of her moons.

Ameen Rihani.

PREFACE.

When Christendom was groping amid the superstitions of the Dark Ages, and the Norsemen were ravaging the western part of Europe, and the princes of Islam were cutting each other's throats in the name of Allah and his Prophet, Abu'l-Ala'l-Ma'arri was waging his bloodless war against the follies and evils of his age. He attacked the superstitions and false traditions of law and religion, proclaiming the supremacy of the mind; he hurled his trenchant invectives at the tyranny, the bigotry, and the quackery of his times, asserting the supremacy of the soul; he held the standard of reason high above that of authority, fighting to the end the battle of the human intellect. An intransigeant with the exquisite mind of a sage and scholar, his weapons were never idle. But he was, above all, a poet; for when he stood before the eternal mystery of Life and Death, he sheathed his sword and murmured a prayer.

Abu'l-Ala'l-Ma'arri,[1] the Lucretius of Islam, the Voltaire of the East, was born in the spring of the year 973 A.D., in the obscure village of Ma'arrah,[2] which is about eighteen hours' journey south of Halab (Aleppo). And instead of Ahmad ibn Abdallah ibn Sulaiman ut-Tanukhi (of the tribe of Tanukh), he was called Abu'l-Ala (the Father of the Sublime), by which patronymic of distinction he is popularly known throughout the Arabic speaking world.

When a boy, Abu'l-Ala was instructed by his father; and subsequently he was sent to Halab, where he pursued his studies under the tutelage of the grammarian Muhammad ibn Abdallah ibn us-Sad. His literary proclivity was evinced in his boyhood, and he wrote verse, we are told, before he was ten. Of these juvenile pieces, however, nothing was preserved.

He was about five years old when he fell a victim to small-pox and almost lost his sight from it. But a weakness in his eyes continued to trouble him and he became, in middle age, I presume, totally blind.[3] Some of his biographers would have us believe he was born blind; others state that he completely lost his sight when he was attacked by the virulent disease; and a few intimate that he could see slightly at least with the right eye. As to whether or not he was blind when he was sent to Halab to pursue his studies, his biographers do not agree. My theory, based on the careful perusal of his poems and on a statement advanced by one of his biographers,[4] is that he lost his sight gradually, and total blindness must have come upon him either in his youth or his middle age.[5] Were we to believe that he was born blind or that he suffered the complete loss of his sight in his boyhood, we should be at a loss to know, not how he wrote his books, for that was done by dictation; not how he taught his pupils, for that was done by lectures; but how he himself was taught in the absence in those days of a regular system of instruction for the blind.

In 1010 A.D. he visited Baghdad, the centre of learning and intelligence and the capital of the Abbaside Khalifs, where he passed about two years and became acquainted with most of the literary men of the age.[6] He attended the lectures and the readings of the leading doctors and grammarians, meeting with a civil reception at the hand of most of them.

He also journeyed to Tripoli,[7] which boasted, in those days, of many public libraries; and, stopping at Ladhekiyah, he lodged in a monastery where he met and befriended a very learned monk. They discussed theology and metaphysics, digressing now and then into the profane. Indeed, the skepticism which permeates Abu'l-Ala's writings must have been nursed in that convent by both the monk and the poet.

These are virtually the only data extant showing the various sources of Abu'l-Ala's learning; but to one endowed with a keen perception, a powerful intellect, a prodigious memory, together with strong innate literary predilections, they seem sufficient. He was especially noted for the extraordinary memory he possessed; and around this our Arab biographers and historians weave a thick net of anecdotes, or rather fables. I have no doubt that one with such a prodigious memory could retain in a few minutes what the average person could not; but when we are told that Abu'l-Ala once heard one of his pupils speaking with a friend in a foreign tongue, and repeated there and then the long conversation, word for word, without having the slightest idea of its meaning, we are disposed to be skeptical. Many such anecdotes are recorded and quoted by his Arab biographers without as much as intimating a single doubt.[8] The fact that he was blind partly explains the abnormal development of his memory.

His career as poet and scholar dates from the time he returned from Baghdad. This, so far as is known, was the last journey he made; and his home became henceforth his earthly prison. He calls himself "A double-fettered Captive,"[9] his solitude being the one and his blindness the other. Like most of the scholars of his age, in the absence of regular educational institutions, with perhaps one or two exceptions, he had to devote a part of his time to the large number of pupils that flocked to Ma'arrah from all parts of Asia Minor, Arabia, and India. Aside from this, he dictated to his numerous amanuenses on every possible and known subject. He is not only a poet of the first rank, but an essayist, a literary critic, and a mathematician as well. Everything he wrote was transcribed by many of his admirers, as was the fashion then, and thus circulated far and near. Nothing, however, was preserved but his Diwans, his Letters and the Epistle of Forgiveness,[10] of which I shall yet have occasion to speak.[11]

His reputation as poet and scholar had now, after his return from Baghdad, overleaped the horizons, as one writer has it. Honors were conferred upon him successively by the rulers and the scholars of his age. His many noted admirers were in constant communication with him. He was now looked upon as "the master of the learned, the chief of the wise, and the sole monarch of the bards of his century." Ma'arrah[12] became the Mecca of every literary aspirant; ambitious young scholars came there for enlightenment and inspiration. And Abu'l-Ala, although a pessimist, received them with his wonted kindness and courtesy. He imparted to them what he knew, and told them candidly what he would not teach, since, unlike other philosophers, he was not able to grasp the truth, nor compass the smallest of the mysteries of creation. In his latter days, youthful admirers sought his blessing, which he, as the childless father of all, graciously conferred, but with no self-assumed spiritual or temporal authority.

For thirty years he remained a vegetarian, living the life of an ascetic.[13] This mode of living led his enemies to accuse him of renouncing Islam and embracing Brahminism, one of the tenets of which forbids the slaughter of animals. The accusation was rather sustained by the dispassionate attitude he held towards it, and, furthermore, by his vehement denunciation of the barbarous practice of killing animals for food or for sport.

Most of the censors of Abu'l-Ala were either spurred to their task by bigotry or animated by jealousy and ignorance. They held him up to ridicule and opprobrium, and such epithets as heretic, atheist, renegade, etc., were freely applied. But he was supremely indifferent to them all,[14] and never would he cross swords with any particular individual; he attacked the false doctrines they were teaching, turning a deaf ear to the virulent vituperations they hurled upon him. I fail to find in the three volumes of his poems, even in the Letters, one acrimonious line savoring of personality.

Ibn-Khillikan, The Plutarch of Arabia, who is

cautious and guarded in his statements, speaking of Abu'l-Ala, truly says:

"His asceticism, his deep sense of right and wrong, his powerful intellect, his prodigious memory, and his wide range of learning, are alike acknowledged by both friend and foe."

His pessimism was natural, in part hereditary. The man was nothing if not genuine and sincere. Ruthlessly he said what he thought and felt. He had no secrets to hide from the world, no thoughts which he dared not express. His soul was as open as Nature; his mind was the polished mirror of his age.[15] It may be that had he not been blind-stricken and had not small-pox disfigured his features, he might have found a palliative in human society. His pessimism might not have been cured, but it might have been rendered at least enticing. Good-fellowship might have robbed it of its sting. Nor is his strong aversion to marriage, in view of these facts, surprising.

He lived to know that "his fame spread from the sequestered village of Ma'arrah to the utmost confines of the Arabic speaking world." In the spring of 1055 A.D. he died, and was buried in a garden surrounding his home. Adh-Dhahabi states that there were present at his grave eighty poets, and that the Koran was read there two hundred times in a fortnight. Eighty poets in the small town of Ma'arrah sounds incredible. But we must bear in mind that almost every one who studies the Arabic grammar has also to study prosody and versification and thus become at least a rhymster. Even to-day, the death of a noted person among the Arabs, is always an occasion for the display of much eloquence and tears, both in prose and verse.

Abu'l-Ala, beside being a poet and scholar of the first rank, was also one of the foremost thinkers of his age. Very little is said of his teachings, his characteristics, his many-sided intellect, in the biographies I have read. The fact that he was a liberal thinker, a trenchant writer,—free, candid, downright, independent, skeptical withal,—answers for the neglect on the part of Mohammedan doctors, who, when they do discuss him, try to conceal from the world what his poems unquestionably reveal. I am speaking, of course, of the neglect after his death. For during his life-time he was much honored, as I have shown, and many distinguished travellers came especially to Ma'arrah to see him. He was also often called upon to act as intercessor with the Emirs for the natives of his village.[16]

The larger collection of his poems, the Luzumiyat,[17] was published in Cairo, in two volumes, by Azeez Zind, from an original Ms. written in the twelfth century, under Abu'l-Ala's own title *Luzum ma la Yalzam*, or the Necessity of what is Unnecessary. This title refers to the special system of rhyming which the poet adopted. And the poems, published in desultory fashion, were written, it seems, at different periods of his life, and are arranged according to his particular alphabetical system of rhyming. They bear no titles except, "And he also says, rhyming with so and so," whatever the consonant and vowel may be. In his Preface to the Luzumiyat he says:

"It happened that I composed these poems during the past years, and in them I have always aimed at the truth. They are certainly free from the blandishments of exaggeration. And while some of them are written in glorification of God, who is above such glory, others are, as it were, a reminder to those who forget, a pinch to those who sleep, and a warning to the children of the earth against the wiles of the great world, where human rights and human gratitude are often strangled by the same hand of Fate."

As for the translation of these chosen quatrains, let me say at the outset that it is almost impossible to adhere to the letter thereof and convey the meaning without being insipid, dull, and at times even ridiculous. There being no affinity between the Arabic and the English, their standards of art and beauty widely differ, and in the process of transformation the outer garment at times must necessarily be doffed. I have always adhered to the spirit, however, preserving the native imagery where it was not too clannish or grotesque. I have added nothing that was foreign to the ruling idea, nor have I omitted anything that was necessary to the completion of the general thought. One might get an idea of what is called a scholarly translation from the works of any of the Orientalists who have made a study of Abu'l-Ala. The first English scholar to mention the poet, as far as I know, was J. D. Carlisle, who in his "Specimens of Arabic Poetry", published in 1810, has paraphrased in verse a quatrain on Pride and Virtue. He also translated into Latin one of Abu'l-Ala's bold epigrams, fearing, I suppose, to publish it at that time in English.

The quatrains which are here published are culled from the three Volumes of his poems, and they are arranged, as nearly as may be, in the logical order of their sequence of thought. They form a kind of eclogue, which the poet-philosopher delivers from his prison in Ma'arrah.

Once, in Damascus, I visited, with some friends, a distinguished Sufi; and when the tea was being served, our host held forth on the subject of Abu'l-Ala's creed. He quoted from the Luzumiyat to show that the poet-philosopher of Ma'arrah was a true Sufi, and of the highest order. "In his passionate hatred of the vile world and all the vile material manifestations of life," quoth our host, "he was like a dervish dancing in sheer bewilderment; a holy man, indeed, melting in tears before the distorted image of Divinity. In his aloofness, as in the purity of his spirit, the ecstatic negations of

Abu'l-Ala can only be translated in terms of the Sufi's creed. In his raptures, *shathat*, he was as distant as Ibn ul-Arabi; and in his bewilderment, *heirat*, he was as deeply intoxicated as Ibn ul-Fared. If others have symbolized the Divinity in wine, he symbolized it in Reason, which is the living oracle of the Soul; he has, in a word, embraced Divinity under the cover of a philosophy of extinction."...

This, and more such from our Sufi host, to which the guests gently nodded understanding. One of them, a young poet and scholar, even added that most of the irreligious opinions that are found in the Luzumiyat were forced upon the poet by the rigorous system of rhyming he adopted. The Rhyme, then, is responsible for the heresies of Abu'l-Ala! Allah be praised! But this view of the matter was not new to me. I have heard it expressed by zealous Muslim scholars, who see in Abu'l-Ala an adversary too strong to be allowed to enlist with the enemy. They will keep him, as one of the "Pillars of the Faith," at any cost. Coming from them, therefore, this rhyme-begotten heresy theory is not surprising.

But I am surprised to find a European scholar like Professor Margoliouth giving countenance to such views; even repeating, to support his own argument,[18] such drivel. For if the system of rhyme-ending imposes upon the poet his irreligious opinions, how can we account for them in his prose writings? How, for instance, explain his book "*Al-fusul wal Ghayat*" (The Chapters and the Purposes), a work in which he parodied the Koran itself, and which only needed, as he said, to bring it to the standard of the Book, "the polishing of four centuries of reading in the pulpit?" And how account for his "*Risalat ul-Ghufran*" (Epistle of Forgiveness), a most remarkable work both in form and conception?—a Divina Comedia in its cotyledonous state, as it were, only that Abu'l-Ala does not seem to have relished the idea of visiting Juhannam. He must have felt that in his "three earthly prisons" he had had enough of it. So he visits the Jannat and there meets the pagan bards of Arabia lulling themselves in eternal bliss under the eternal shades of the *sidr* tree, writing and reading and discussing poetry. Now, to people the Muslim's Paradise with heathen poets who have been forgiven,—hence the title of the Work,—and received among the blest,—is not this clear enough, bold enough, loud enough even for the deaf and the blind? "The idea," says Professor Nicholson, speaking of The Epistle of Forgiveness,[19] "is carried out with such ingenuity and in a spirit of audacious burlesque that reminds one of Lucien."

This does not mean, however, that the work is essentially of a burlesque quality. Abu'l-Ala had humor; but his earnest tone is never so little at an ebb as when he is in his happiest mood. I quote from The Epistle of Forgiveness:

"Sometimes you may find a man skilful in his trade," says the Author, "perfect in sagacity and in the use of arguments, but when he comes to religion he is found obstinate, so does he follow in the old groove. Piety is implanted in human nature; it is deemed a sure refuge. To the growing child, that which falls from his elders' lips is a lesson that abides with him all his life. Monks in their cloisters and devotees in their mosques accept their creed just as a story is handed down from him who tells it, without distinguishing between a true interpreter and a false. If one of these had found his kin among the Magians, or among the Sabians, he would have become nearly or quite like them."

It does seem, too, that the strain of heterodoxy in Abu'l-Ala is partly hereditary. His father, who was also a poet of some distinction, and his maternal uncle, were both noted for their liberal opinions in religious matters. And he himself, alluding in one of his poems to those who reproached him for not making the pilgrimage to Mecca, says that neither his father, nor his cousin, nor his uncle had pilgrimaged at all, and that he will not be denied forgiveness, if they are forgiven. And if they are not, he had as lief share their fate.

But aside from his prose writings, in which, do what we may, we can not explain away his supposed heresies, we find in the Luzumiyat themselves his dominant ideas on religion, for instance, being a superstition; wine, an unmitigated evil; virtue, its own reward; the cremation of the dead, a virtue; the slaughter or even the torture of animals a crime;[20] doubt, a way to truth; reason, the only prophet and guide;—we find these ideas clothed in various images and expressed in varied forms, but unmistakable in whatever guise we find them. Here, for instance, is Professor Nicholson's almost literal translation of a quatrain from the Luzumiyat:

> Hanifs[21] are stumbling,
>   Christians gone astray,
> Jews wildered, Magians far
>   on error's way:—
> We mortals are composed
>   of two great schools,
> Enlightened knaves or else
>   religious fools.

And here is the same idea, done in a large picture. The translation, literal too, is mine:

> 'Tis strange that Kusrah
>   and his people wash
> Their faces in the staling of
>   the kine;
> And that the Christians say,
>   Almighty God

Was tortured, mocked, and
    crucified in fine:
And that the Jews should
    picture Him as one
Who loves the odor of a
    roasting chine;
And stranger still that
    Muslems travel far
To kiss a black stone said to
    be divine:—
Almighty God! will all the
    human race
Stray blindly from the
    Truth's most sacred
    shrine?[22]

The East still remains the battle-ground of the creeds. And the Europeans, though they shook off *their* fetters of moral and spiritual slavery, would keep us in ours to facilitate the conquests of European commence. Thus the terrible Dragon, which is fed by the foreign missionary and the native priest, by the theologians and the ulama, and which still preys upon the heart and mind of Orient nations, is as active to-day as it was ten centuries ago. Let those consider this, who think Von Kremer exaggerated when he said, "Abu'l-Ala is a poet many centuries ahead of his time."

Before closing, I wish to call attention to a question which, though unimportant in itself, is nevertheless worthy of the consideration of all admirers of Arabic and Persian literature. I refer to the similarity of thought which exists between Omar Khayyam and Abu'l-Ala. The former, I have reason to believe, was an imitator or a disciple of the latter. The birth of the first poet and the death of the second are not very far apart: they both occurred about the middle of the eleventh century. The English reading public here and abroad has already formed its opinion of Khayyam. Let it not, therefore, be supposed that in making this claim I aim to shake or undermine its great faith. My desire is to confirm, not to weaken,—to expand, not contract,—the Oriental influence on the Occidental mind.

Whoever will take the trouble, however, to read Omar Khayyam in conjunction with what is here translated of Abu'l-Ala, can not fail to see the striking similarity in thought and image of certain phases of the creed or the lack of creed of both poets.[23] To be sure, the skepticism and pessimism of Omar are to a great extent imported from Ma'arrah. But the Arab philosopher in his religious opinions is far more outspoken than the Persian tent-maker. I do not say that Omar was a plagiarist; but I say this: just as Voltaire, for instance, acquired most of his liberal and skeptical views from Hobbes, Locke and Bayle, so did Omar acquire his from Abu'l-Ala. In my notes to these quatrains I have quoted in comparison from both the Fitzgerald and the Herron-Allen versions of the Persian poet; and with so much or so little said, I leave the matter in the hands of the reader, who, upon a careful examination, will doubtless bear me out as to this point.

---

1. My learned friend, Count E. de Mulinen, called my attention to the work of Von Kremer on Abu'l-Ala. And I have seen copies of a certain German Asiatic Review in which were published translations, made by that eminent Orientalist, of many poems from the Luzumiyat. He speaks of Abu'l-Ala as one of the greatest moralists of all times, whose profound genius anticipated much that is commonly attributed to the so-called modern spirit of enlightenment.

   Professor D. S. Margoliouth has also translated into English the Letters of Abu'l-Ala, which were published with the Arabic Text at the Clarendon Press, Oxford, 1898. Also Professor Raynold A. Nicholson, in his work, "A Literary History of the Arabs," discusses the poet at length and renders into English some poems from the Luzumiyat. A work was published by Charles Carrington, Paris, 1904, under the title, "Un Précurseur d'Omar Khayyam, Le Poéte Aveugle: Extraits de Poémes et de Lettres d'Abu'l-Ala al-Ma'arri." And another, "The Diwan of Abu'l-Ala," done into English by Henry Baerlein, who must have helped himself freely to the Quatrains of Von Kremer.

2. For a picturesque description of the squalidness and sordidness of Ma'arrah and its people, see Letter XX of "The Letters of Abu'l-Ala," Oxford Edition.

3. When he visited Baghdad he was about thirty-seven years of age. And when he went to attend a lecture there by one of the leading scholars, he was called by the lecturer, *istabl*, which is Syrian slang for blind.

4. "He was four years of age when he had the attack of small-pox. The sight of his left eye was entirely lost and the eyeball of his right had turned white. Al-Hafiz us-Silafi relates: 'Abu Muhammad Abdallah told me that he visited him (Abu'l-Ala) once with his uncle and found him sitting on an old hair matting. He was very old, and the disease that attacked him in his boyhood had left its deep traces on his emaciated face. He bade me come near him and blessed me as he placed his hand on my head. I was a boy then, and I can picture him before me now. I looked into his eyes and remarked how the one was horribly protruding, and the other, buried in its socket, could barely be seen.'"—Ibn Khillikan.

5. "How long he retained any sort of vision is not certain. His frequent references in his writings to stars, flowers, and the forms of the Arabic letters imply that he could see a little at least some years after this calamity."—D. S. Margoliouth: The Letters of Abu'l-Ala.

   "He used to play chess and *nard*."—Safadi.

6. For an interesting account of Literary Society in Baghdad see Renan's "Islam and Science"; also the Biography to the Letters of Abu'l-Ala. Prof. Margoliouth, though not unfair in his judgment of the poet, is unnecessarily captious at times. He would seem partial to the suffrage of orthodox Mohammedans with regard to Abu'l-Ala's unorthodox religious views. But they have a reason, these ulama, for endeavoring to keep a genius like Abu'l-Ala within the pale of belief. Which reason, let us hope, has no claim on Prof. Margoliouth. And in his attempt to depreciate Abu'l-Ala as a disinterested and independent scholar and poet, he does not escape the inconsistency which often follows in the wake of cavil. Read this, for instance:

   "Like many of those who have failed to secure material prosperity, he found comfort in a system which flatters the vanity of those who have not succeeded by teaching that success is not worth attaining."

   And this, not on the same page perhaps, but close to it:

"For though other roads towards obtaining the means of supporting himself at Baghdad have been open to him, *that which he refused to follow* (the profession of an encomiast, *i. e.* a sycophant, a toady) was the most certain."

7. Biography of Abu'l-Ala by Adh-Dhahabi.
8. "The Letters, which abound in quotations, enable us to gauge the power of his memory better than these wonder-loving narrators."—D. S. Margoliouth.
9. In one of his poems he speaks of three prisons, his body being the third. Here is Professor Nicholson's translation:

> Methink I am thrice-imprisoned—ask not me
> Of news that need no telling—
> By loss of sight, confinement in my house,
> And this vile body for my spirit's dwelling.

10. Also his Commentary on the works of the poet Al-Mutanabbi.
11. Adh-Dhahabi gives the titles of forty-eight of his works, to which Safadi adds fourteen. A literary baggage of considerable bulk, had not most of it perished when the Crusaders took Ma'arrah in 1098. Now, the Luzumiyat, the Letters, Suct uz-Zand and the Epistle of Forgiveness can be obtained in printed form.
12. "What he says of Al-Maghribi in the First Letter became literally true of himself: 'As Sinai derives its fame from Moses and the Stone from Abraham, so Ma'arrah is from this time (after his return from Baghdad) known by him.'"—D. S. Margoliouth.
13. Even before he visited Baghdad he had a pension of thirty dinars (about $100), half of which he paid to his servant, and the other half was sufficient to secure for him the necessaries of life. "He lived on lentils and figs," says Adh-Dhahabi; "he slept on a felt mattress; he wore nothing but cotton garments; and his dwelling was furnished with a straw matting."
14. We have the following from Adh-Dhahabi:

"One of these critics came one day to Abu'l-Ala and relating the conversation himself said, 'What is it that is quoted and said about you?' I asked.

'It is false; they are jealous of me,' he replied.

'And what have you to incite their jealousy? You have left for them both this world and the other.'

'And the other?' murmured the poet, questioning, ruminating. 'And the other, too?'"

15. "His poems, generally known as the Luzumiyat, arrest attention by their boldness and originality as well as by the sombre and earnest tone which pervades them."—Raynold A. Nicholson: A Literary History of the Arabs.

16. The Governor of Halab, Salih ibn Mirdas, passed once by Ma'arrah, when thirty of its distinguished citizens were imprisoned on account of a riot in the town the previous year. Abu'l-Ala being asked to intercede for them, was led to Salih, who received him most politely and asked him what he desired. The poet, in eloquent but unflattering speech, asked Salih 'to take and give forgiveness.' And the Governor, not displeased, replied: 'I grant it you.' Whereupon the prisoners were released.

17. "His poems leave no aspect of the age (in which he lived) untouched, and present a vivid picture of degeneracy and corruption, in which tyrannous rulers, venal judges, hypocritical and unscrupulous theologians, swindling astrologers, roving swarms of dervishes and godless Carmathians, occupy a prominent place."—Raynold A. Nicholson: A Literary History of the Arabs.

18. "The Mohammedan critics who thought he let his opinions be guided by his pen probably came near the truth. And any man who writes in such fetters as the meter (he means the rhyme-ending; for Abu'l-Ala made use of every known meter of Arabic prosody) of the Luzumiyat imposes, can exercise but slight control over his thoughts."—D. S. Margoliouth: Letters of Abu'l-Ala.

19. This work, of which Professor Nicholson says there are but two copies extant, one in Constantinople and the other in his own Collection, was published in Cairo, in 1907, edited by Sheikh Ibrahim ul-Yazeji.

20. "To let go a flea is a more virtuous act than to give a dirham to a beggar."—Abu'l-Ala.

21. The Orthodox, *i. e.* the Mohammedans.

22. I do not find these verses in the printed copies of either the Luzumiyat or Suct uz-Zand. But they are quoted, from some Ms. copy I suppose, by the historian Abu'l-Fida.

23. Omar wrote poetry in Arabic too. My learned friend, Isa Iskandar Maluf of Zehleh, Mt. Lebanon, showed me some quatrains of "Omar the Tent-maker and Astronomer," in an old Arabic Ms. which bear a striking resemblance to some of Abu'l-Ala's both in thought and style.

THE LUZUMIYAT OF ABU'L-ALA

I

The sable wings of Night pursuing day
    Across the opalescent hills, display
    The wondrous star-gems which the fiery suns
    Are scattering upon their fiery way.[1]

II

O my Companion, Night is passing fair,
    Fairer than aught the dawn and sundown wear;
    And fairer, too, than all the gilded days
    Of blond Illusion and its golden snare.

III

Hark, in the minarets muazzens call
The evening hour that in the interval
Of darkness Ahmad might remembered be,—
Remembered of the Darkness be they all.[2]

IV

And hear the others who with cymbals try
To stay the feet of every passer-by:
The market-men along the darkling lane
Are crying up their wares.—Oh! let them cry.[3]

V

Mohammed or Messiah! Hear thou me,
The truth entire nor here nor there can be;
How should our God who made the sun and moon
Give all his light to One, I cannot see.

VI

Come, let us with the naked Night now rest
And read in Allah's Book the sonnet best:
The Pleiads—ah, the Moon from them departs,—
She draws her veil and hastens toward the west.

VII

The Pleiads follow; and our Ethiop Queen,
Emerging from behind her starry screen,
Will steep her tresses in the saffron dye
Of dawn, and vanish in the morning sheen.[4]

VIII

The secret of the day and night is in
The constellations, which forever spin
Around each other in the comet-dust;—
The comet-dust and humankind are kin.

IX

But whether of dust or fire or foam, the glaive
Of Allah cleaves the planet and the wave
Of this mysterious Heaven-Sea of life,
And lo! we have the Cradle of the Grave.

X

The Grave and Cradle, the untiring twain,
Who in the markets of this narrow lane
Bordered of darkness, ever give and take
In equal measure—what's the loss or gain?

XI

Ay, like the circles which the sun doth spin
Of gossamer, we end as we begin;
Our feet are on the heads of those that pass,
But ever their Graves around our Cradles grin.

XII

And what avails it then that Man be born
To joy or sorrow?—why rejoice or mourn?
The doling doves are calling to the rose;
The dying rose is bleeding o'er the thorn.

XIII

And he the Messenger, who takes away
The faded garments, purple, white, and gray
Of all our dreams unto the Dyer, will
Bring back new robes to-morrow—so they
say.[5]

XIV

But now the funeral is passing by,
And in its trail, beneath this moaning sky,
The howdaj comes,—both vanish into night;
To me are one, the sob, the joyous cry.[6]

XV

With   tombs   and   ruined   temples   groans
the land
   In which our forbears in the drifting sand
   Arise as dunes upon the track of Time
   To mark the cycles of the moving hand

XVI

   Of Fate. Alas! and we shall follow soon
   Into the night eternal or the noon;
   The wayward daughters of the spheres return
   Unto the bosom of their sun or moon.

XVII

   And from the last days of Thamud and 'Ad
   Up to the first of Hashem's fearless lad,
   Who smashed the idols of his mighty tribe,
   What idols and what heroes Death has had![7]

XVIII

   Tread lightly, for the mighty that have been
   Might now be breathing in the dust unseen;
   Lightly, the violets beneath thy feet
   Spring   from   the   mole   of   some   Arabian
queen.[8]

<h1 style="text-align:center">XIX</h1>

Many a grave embraces friend and foe
Behind the curtain of this sorry show
Of love and hate inscrutable; alas!
The Fates will always reap the while they sow.

<h1 style="text-align:center">XX</h1>

The silken fibre of the fell Zakkum,
As warp and woof, is woven on the loom
Of life into a tapestry of dreams
To decorate the chariot-seat of Doom.[9]

<h1 style="text-align:center">XXI</h1>

And still we weave, and still we are content
In slaving for the sovereigns who have spent
The savings of the toiling of the mind
Upon the glory of Dismemberment.

<h1 style="text-align:center">XXII</h1>

Nor king nor slave the hungry Days will spare;
Between their fangéd Hours alike we fare:
Anon they bound upon us while we play
Unheeding at the threshold of their Lair.

XXIII

Then Jannat or Juhannam? From the height
Of reason I can see nor fire nor light
That feeds not on the darknesses; we pass
From world to world, like shadows through the
night. [10]

XXIV

Or sleep—and shall it be eternal sleep
Somewhither in the bosom of the deep
Infinities of cosmic dust, or here
Where gracile cypresses the vigil keep!

XXV

Upon the threshing-floor of life I burn
Beside the Winnower a word to learn;
And only this: Man's of the soil and sun,
And to the soil and sun he shall return.

XXVI

And like a spider's house or sparrow's nest,
The Sultan's palace, though upon the crest
Of glory's mountain, soon or late must go:
Ay, all abodes to ruin are addrest.

XXVII

So, too, the creeds of Man: the one prevails
Until the other comes; and this one fails
When that one triumphs; ay, the lonesome
world
Will always want the latest fairy-tales.

XXVIII

Seek not the Tavern of Belief, my friend,
Until the Sakis there their morals mend;
A lie imbibed a thousand lies will breed,
And thou'lt become a Saki in the end.

XXIX

By fearing whom I trust I find my way
To truth; by trusting wholly I betray
The trust of wisdom; better far is doubt
Which brings the false into the light of day. [11]

XXX

Or wilt thou commerce have with those
who make
Rugs of the rainbow, rainbows of the snake,
Snakes of a staff, and other wondrous things?

———

The burning thirst a mirage can not slake.

XXXI

Religion is a maiden veiled in prayer,
Whose bridal gifts and dowry those who care
Can buy in Mutakallem's shop of words
But I for such, a dirham can not spare.[12]

XXXII

Why linger here, why turn another page?
Oh! seal with doubt the whole book of
the age;
Doubt every one, even him, the seeming slave
Of righteousness, and doubt the canting sage.

XXXIII

Some day the weeping daughters of Hadil
Will say unto the bulbuls: "Let's appeal
To Allah in behalf of Brother Man
Who's at the mercy now of Ababil."[13]

XXXIV

Of Ababil! I would the tale were true,—
Would all the birds were such winged
furies too;
The scourging and the purging were a boon
For me, O my dear Brothers, and for you.

XXXV

Methinks Allah divides me to complete
His problem, which with Xs is replete;
For I am free and I am too in chains
Groping along the labyrinthine street.

XXXVI

And round the Well how oft my Soul doth grope
  Athirst; but lo! my Bucket hath no Rope:
  I cry for water, and the deep, dark Well
Echoes my wailing cry, but not my hope.

XXXVII

Ah, many have I seen of those who fell
  While drawing, with a swagger, from the Well;
  They came with Rope and Bucket, and they went
Empty of hand another tale to tell.

XXXVIII

The *I* in me standing upon the brink
  Would leap into the Well to get a drink;
  But how to rise once in the depth, I cry,
And cowardly behind my logic slink.[14]

XXXIX

And she: "How long must I the burden bear?
How long this tattered garment must I wear?"
And I: "Why wear it? Leave it here, and go
Away without it—little do I care."

XL

But once when we were quarreling, the door
Was opened by a Visitor who bore
Both Rope and Pail; he offered them and said:
"Drink, if you will, but once, and nevermore."

XLI

One draught, more bitter than the Zakkum
tree,
	Brought us unto the land of mystery
	Where rising Sand and Dust and Flame
conceal
	The door of every Caravanseri.

XLII

We reach a door and there the legend find.
"To all the Pilgrims of the Human Mind:
Knock and pass on!" We knock and knock and
knock;
But no one answers save the moaning wind.

XLIII

How like a door the knowledge we attain,
Which door is on the bourne of the Inane;
It opens and our nothingness is closed,—
It closes and in darkness we remain.

XLIV

Hither we come unknowing, hence we go;
Unknowing we are messaged to and fro;
And yet we think we know all things of earth
And sky—the suns and stars we think we
know.

XLV

Apply thy wit, O Brother, here and there
Upon this and upon that; but beware
Lest in the end—ah, better at the start
Go to the Tinker for a slight repair.

XLVI

And why so much ado, and wherefore lay
The burden of the years upon the day
Of thy vain dreams? Who polishes his sword
Morning and eve will polish it away.

XLVII

I heard it whispered in the cryptic streets
Where every sage the same dumb shadow
meets:
"We are but words fallen from the lipe of Time
Which God, that we might understand,
repeats."

XLVIII

Another said: "The creeping worm hath
shown,
In her discourse on human flesh and bone,
That Man was once the bed on which she
slept—
The walking dust was once a thing of
stone."[15]

XLIX

And still another: "We are coins which fade
In circulation, coins which Allah made
To cheat Iblis: the good and bad alike
Are spent by Fate upon a passing shade."[16]

L

And in the pottery the potter cried,
As on his work shone all the master's pride—

"How is it, Rabbi, I, thy slave, can make
Such vessels as nobody dare deride?"[17]

LI

The Earth then spake: "My children silent be;
Same are to God the camel and the flea:
He makes a mess of me to nourish you,
Then makes a mess of you to nourish me."

LII

Now, I believe the Potter will essay
Once more the Wheel, and from a better clay
Will make a better Vessel, and perchance
A masterpiece which will endure for aye.

LIII

With better skill he even will remould
The scattered potsherds of the New and Old;
Then you and I will not disdain to buy,
Though in the mart of Iblis they be sold.

LIV

Sooth I have told the masters of the mart
Of rusty creeds and Babylonian art
Of magic. Now the truth about myself—
Here is the secret of my wincing heart.

LV

I muse, but in my musings I recall
The days of my iniquity; we're all—
An arrow shot across the wilderness,
Somewhither, in the wilderness must fall.

LVI

I laugh, but in my laughter-cup I pour
The tears of scorn and melancholy sore;
I who am shattered by the hand of Doubt,
Like glass to be remoulded nevermore.[18]

LVII

I wheedle, too, even like my slave Zeidun,
Who robs at dawn his brother, and at noon
Prostrates himself in prayer—ah, let us pray
That Night might blot us and our sins, and
soon.[19]

LVIII

But in the fatal coils, without intent,
We sin; wherefore a future punishment?
They say the metal dead a deadly steel
Becomes with Allah's knowledge and consent.

LIX

And even the repentant sinner's tear
Falling into Juhannam's very ear,
Goes to its heart, extinguishes its fire
For ever and forever,—so I hear.

LX

Between the white and purple Words of Time
In motley garb with Destiny I rhyme:
The colored glasses to the water give
The colors of a symbolry sublime.

LXI

How   oft,   when   young,   my   brothers   I
would shun
If their religious feelings were not spun
Of my own cobweb, which I find was but
A spider's revelation of the sun.

LXII

Now, mosques and churches—even a Kaaba
Stone,
Korans and Bibles—even a martyr's bone,—
All these and more my heart can tolerate,
For my religion's love, and love alone.[20]

LXIII

To humankind, O Brother, consecrate
Thy heart, and shun the hundred Sects that
prate
About the things they little know about—
Let all receive thy pity, none thy hate.

LXIV

The tavern and the temple also shun,
For sheikh and libertine in sooth are one;
And when the pious knave begins to pule,
The knave in purple breaks his vow anon.

LXV

"The wine's forbidden," say these honest folk,
But for themselves the law they will revoke;
The snivelling sheikh says he's without a garb,
When in the tap-house he had pawned his
cloak.

LXVI

Or in the house of lust. The priestly name
And priestly turban once were those of
Shame—
And Shame is preaching in the pulpit now—
If pulpits tumble down, I'm not to blame.

LXVII

For after she declaims upon the vows
Of Faith, she pusillanimously bows
Before the Sultan's wine-empurpled throne,
While he and all his courtezans carouse.

LXVIII

Carouse, ye sovereign lords! The wheel will roll
Forever to confound and to console:
Who sips to-day the golden cup will drink
Mayhap to-morrow in a wooden bowl—

LXIX

And silent drink. The tumult of our mirth
Is worse than our mad welcoming of birth:—
The thunder hath a grandeur, but the rains,
Without the thunder, quench the thirst of Earth.

LXX

The Prophets, too, among us come to teach,
Are one with those who from the pulpit preach;
They pray, and slay, and pass away, and yet
Our ills are as the pebbles on the beach.

LXXI

And   though   around   the   temple   they
should run
    For seventy times and seven, and in the sun
    Of mad devotion drool, their prayers are still
    Like their desires of feasting-fancies spun.

LXXII

Oh! let them in the marshes grope, or ride
Their jaded Myths along the mountain-side;
Come up with me, O Brother, to the heights
Where Reason is the prophet and the guide.

LXXIII

"What is thy faith and creed," they ask of me,
"And who art thou? Unseal thy pedigree."—
I am the child of Time, my tribe, mankind,
And now this world's my caravanseri.

LXXIV

Swathe thee in wool, my Sufi friend, and go
Thy way; in cotton I the wiser grow;
But we ourselves are shreds of earth, and soon
The Tailor of the Universe will sew.

LXXV

Ay! suddenly the mystic Hand will seal
The saint's devotion and the sinner's weal;
They worship Saturn, but I worship One
Before whom Saturn and the Heavens kneel.

LXXVI

Among the crumbling ruins of the creeds
The Scout upon his camel played his reeds
And called out to his people,—"Let us hence!
The pasture here is full of noxious weeds."

LXXVII

Among us falsehood is proclaimed aloud,
But truth is whispered to the phantom bowed
Of conscience; ay! and Wrong is ever crowned,
While Right and Reason are denied a shroud.[21]

LXXVIII

And why in this dark Kingdom tribute pay?
With clamant multitudes why stop to pray?
Oh! hear the inner Voice:—"If thou'lt be right,
Do what they deem is wrong, and go thy way."

LXXIX

Thy way unto the Sun the spaces through
Where king Orion's black-eyed huris slew
The Mother of Night to guide the Wings that bear
The flame divine hid in a drop of dew.

LXXX

Hear ye who in the dust of ages creep,
And in the halls of wicked masters sleep:—
Arise! and out of this wan weariness
Where Allah's laughter makes the Devil weep.

LXXXI

Arise! for lo! the Laughter and the Weeping
Reveal the Weapon which the Master's keeping
Above your heads; Oh! take it up and strike!
The lion of tyranny is only sleeping.

LXXXII

Evil and Virtue? Shadows on the street
Of Fate and Vanity,—but shadows meet
When in the gloaming they are hast'ning forth
To drink with Night annihilation sweet.

LXXXIII

And thus the Sun will write and will efface
The mystic symbols which the sages trace
In vain, for all the worlds of God are stored
In his enduring vessels Time and Space.

LXXXIV

For all my learning's but a veil, I guess,
Veiling the phantom of my nothingness;
Howbeit, there are those who think me wise,
And those who think me—even these I bless.

LXXXV

And all my years, as vapid as my lay,
Are bitter morsels of a mystic day,—
The day of Fate, who carries in his lap
December snows and snow-white flowers of May.

LXXXVI

Allah, my sleep is woven through, it seems,
With burning threads of night and golden beams;
But when my dreams are evil they come true;
When they are not, they are, alas! but dreams.

LXXXVII

The subtle ways of Destiny I know;
In me she plays her game of "Give and Go."
Misfortune I receive in cash, but joy,
In drafts on Heaven or on the winds that blow.

LXXXVIII

I give and go, grim Destiny,—I play
Upon this checker-board of Night and Day
The dark game with thee, but the day will come
When one will turn the Board the other way.

LXXXIX

If my house-swallow, laboring with zest,
Felt like myself the burden of unrest,
Unlightened by inscrutable designs,
She would not build her young that cozy nest.

XC

Thy life with guiltless life-blood do not stain—
Hunt not the children of the woods; in vain
Thou'lt try one day to wash thy bloody hand:
Nor hunter here nor hunted long remain.[22]

XCI

Oh! cast my dust away from thee, and doff
Thy cloak of sycophancy and like stuff:
I'm but a shadow on the sandy waste,—
Enough of thy duplicity, enough!

XCII

Behold! the Veil that hid thy soul is torn
And all thy secrets on the winds are borne:
The hand of Sin has written on thy face
"Awake, for these untimely furrows warn!"

XCIII

A prince of souls, 'tis sung in ancient lay,
One morning sought a vesture of the clay;
He came into the Pottery, the fool—
The lucky fool was warned to stay away.[23]

XCIV

But I was not. Oh! that the Fates decree
That I now cast aside this clay of me;
My soul and body wedded for a while
Are sick and would that separation be.

XCV

"Thou shalt not kill!"—Thy words, O God,
we heed,
  Though thy two Soul-devouring Angels feed
  Thy Promise of another life on this,—
  To have spared us both, it were a boon
indeed.[24]

XCVI

Oh! that some one would but return to tell
If old Nubakht is burning now in hell,
  Or if the workers for the Prophet's prize
  Are laughing at his Paradisal sell.[25]

XCVII

Once I have tried to string a few Pearl-seeds
Upon my Rosary of wooden beads;
  But I have searched, and I have searched
in vain
  For pearls in all the caverns of the creeds

XCVIII

And in the palaces of wealth I found
Some beads of wisdom scattered on the
ground,
  Around the throne of Power, beneath the feet

Of fair-faced slaves with flowers of folly
crowned.

XCIX

Thy wealth can shed no tears around thy bier,
Nor can it wash thy hands of shame and fear;
Ere thou departest with it freely part,—
Let others plead for thee and God will hear.

C

For me thy silks and feathers have no charm
The pillow I like best is my right arm;
The comforts of this passing show I spurn,
For Poverty can do the soul no harm.

CI

The guiding hand of Allah I can see
Upon my staff: of what use then is he
Who'd be the blind man's guide? Thou
silent oak,
No son of Eve shall walk with me and thee.

CII

My life's the road on which I blindly speed:
My goal's the grave on which I plant a reed
To shape my Hope, but soon the Hand unseen

Will strike, and lo! I'm but a sapless weed.

CIII

O Rabbi, curse us not if we have been
Nursed in the shadow of the Gate of Sin
Built by thy hand—yea, ev'n thine angels blink
When we are coming out and going in.[26]

CIV

And like the dead of Ind I do not fear
To go to thee in flames; the most austere
Angel of fire a softer tooth and tongue
Hath he than dreadful Munker and Nakir.[27]

CV

Now, at this end of Adam's line I stand
Holding my father's life-curse in my hand,
Doing no one the wrong that he did me:—
Ah, would that he were barren as the sand![28]

CVI

Ay, thus thy children, though they sovereigns
be,
When truth upon them dawns, will turn on
thee,
Who cast them into life's dark labyrinth

Where even old Izrail can not see.[29]

CVII

And in the labyrinth both son and sire
Awhile will fan and fuel hatred's fire;
Sparks of the log of evil are all men
Allwhere—extinguished be the race entire!

CVIII

If miracles were wrought in ancient years,
Why not to-day, O Heaven-cradled seers?
The highway's strewn with dead, the lepers
weep,
If ye but knew,—if ye but saw their tears!

CIX

Fan thou a lisping fire and it will leap
In flames, but dost thou fan an ashy heap?
They would respond, indeed, whom thou dost
call,
Were they not dead, alas! or dead asleep.

CX

The way of vice is open as the sky,
The way of virtue's like the needle's eye;
But whether here or there, the eager Soul

Has only two Companions—Whence
and Why.

CXI

Whence come, O firmament, thy myriad
lights?
Whence comes thy sap, O vineyard of the
heights?
Whence comes the perfume of the rose, and
whence
The spirit-larva which the body blights?

CXII

Whence does the nettle get its bitter sting?
Whence do the honey bees their honey bring?
Whence our Companions, too—our Whence
and Why?
O Soul, I do not know a single thing!

CXIII

How many like us in the ages past
Have blindly soared, though like a pebble cast,
Seeking the veil of mystery to tear,
But fell accurst beneath the burning blast?

CXIV

Why try to con the book of earth and sky,
Why seek the truth which neither you nor I
Can grasp? But Death methinks the secret keeps,
And will impart it to us by and by.

CXV

The Sultan, too, relinquishing his throne
Must wayfare through the darkening dust alone
Where neither crown nor kingdom be, and he,
Part of the Secret, here and there is blown.[30]

CXVI

To clay the mighty Sultan must return
And, chancing, help a praying slave to burn
His midnight oil before the face of Him,
Who of the Sultan makes an incense urn.

CXVII

Turned to a cup, who once the sword of state
Held o'er the head of slave and potentate,
Is now held in the tippler's trembling hand,
Or smashed upon the tavern-floor of Fate.

CXVIII

For this I say, Be watchful of the Cage
Of chance; it opes alike to fool and sage;
Spy on the moment, for to-morrow'll be,
Like yesterday, an obliterated page.[31]

CXIX

Yea, kiss the rosy cheeks of new-born Day,
And hail eternity in every ray
Forming a halo round its infant head,
Illumining thy labyrinthine way.

CXX

But I, the thrice-imprisoned, try to troll
Strains of the song of night, which fill
with dole
My blindness, my confinement, and my
flesh—
The sordid habitation of my soul.

CXXI

Howbeit, my inner vision heir shall be
To the increasing flames of mystery
Which may illumine yet my prisons all,
And crown the ever living hope of me.

---

1. To open a poem with a few amatory lines, is a literary tradition among Arab poets. But Abu'l-Ala, having had no occasion to evince such tender emotions, whether real or merely academic, succeeded, as in everything else he did, in deviating from the trodden path. I find, however, in his minor Diwan, *Suct uz-Zand*, a slight manifestation of his youthful ardor, of which this and the succeeding quatrains, descriptive of the charms of Night, are fairly representative.
2. "Ahmad," Mohammed the Prophet.
3. "And hear the others who with cymbals try," etc., meaning the Christians; in the preceding quatrain he referred to the Mohammedans.
4. Milton, in Il Penseroso, also speaks of night as "the starred Ethiop queen"; and Shakespeare, in Romeo and Juliet, has these lines:

    "Her beauty hangs upon the cheek of night
    As a rich jewel in an Ethiop ear."

    The source of inspiration is the same to all world-poets, who only differ sometimes in the jars they bring to the source.
5. The purple, white, and gray garments, symbolizing Man's dreams of power, of love, and of bliss.
6. The same idea is expressed by Omar Khayyam. Here are the first three lines of the 122nd quatrain of Heron-Allen's literal translation:

    "To him who understands the mysteries of the world
    The joy and sorrow of the world is all the same,
    Since the good and the bad of the world all come to an end."

    "Howdaj," a sort of palanquin borne by camels; hence, a wedding or a triumphal procession.
7. "Thamud" and "'Ad," two of the primitive tribes which figure prominently in the legendary history of Arabia. They flouted and stoned the prophets that were sent to them, and are constantly held up in the Koran as terrible examples of the pride that goeth before destruction.

    "Hashem's fearless lad," Mohammed the Prophet.

8. I quote again from Omar, Fitzgerald's translation:
   "And this reviving Herb, whose Tender Green
   Fledges the River-Lip, on which we lean—
   Ah, lean upon it lightly! for who knows
   From what once lovely Lip it springs unseen."
   In justice to both the Persian and the Arab poet, however, I give the 43d quatrain of Heron-Allen's, which I think contains two lines of that of Fitzgerald, together with Abu'l-Ala's own poetic-fancy.
   "Everywhere that there has been a rose or tulip bed
   There has been spilled the crimson blood of a king;
   Every violet shoot that grows from the earth
   Is a mole that was once upon the cheek of beauty."

9. "Zakkum," a tree which, in Mohammedan mythology, is said to have its roots in hell, and from which are fed the dwellers of hell-fire. In one of the Chapters of the Koran, The Saffat, I find this upon it: "And is that a pure bounty, or the Zakkum tree? It is a tree which groweth in hell; its fruits are like unto the heads of the devils, who eat from it, and from it fill their stomachs."
   Zakkum is also one of the bitter-fruited trees of Arabia. And the people there speak of "a mouthful of zakkum" when they want to describe an unhappy experience. It is also the name of one of the plants of the desert, whose flower is like the jasmine; and of one of the trees of Jericho, whose fruit is like the date, but somewhat bitter.

10. "Jannat," Paradise. "Juhannam," Hell.

11. And Tennyson also says:
   "There is more truth in honest doubt,
   Believe me, than in all the creeds."

12. "Mutakallem," disputant. The *mutakallemin* are the logicians and theologians of Islam.

13. Hadil is a poetic term for dove. And in Arabic mythology it is the name of a particular dove, which died of thirst in the days of Noah, and is bemoaned until this day.
   "Ababil," a flock of birds, who scourged with flint-stones which they carried in their beaks, one of the ancient Arab tribes, noted for its idolatry and evil practices.

14. I quote again from Omar, Fitzgerald's version, quatrain
    44:
    "Why, if the Soul can fling the dust aside,
    And naked on the air of Heaven ride,
    Were't not a shame—were't not a shame for him
    In this clay carcass crippled to abide?"
    And from Heron-Allen's, quatrain 145:
    "O Soul, if thou canst purify thyself from the dust of
    the clay,
    Thou, naked spirit, canst soar in the heav'ns,
    The Empyrian is thy sphere—let it be thy shame
    That thou comest and art a dweller within the con-
    fines of earth."
15. "The walking dust was once a thing of stone," is my ren-
    dering of the line,
    "And he concerning whom the world is puzzled
    Is an animal evolved of inorganic matter."
    This line of Abu'l-Ala is much quoted by his enthusi-
    astic admirers of the present day to prove that he antici-
    pated Darwin's theory of evolution. And it is remarkable
    how the fancy of the poet sometimes coincides with the
    logical conclusions of the scientist.
16. "Iblis," the devil.
17. "Rabbi," my lord God.
18. This quatrain is quoted by many of the Biographers of
    Abu'l-Ala to prove that he is a materialist. Which argu-
    ment is easily refuted, however, with others quatrains
    taken at random from the Luzumiyat.
19. Omar was also a confessed cynical-hypocrite. Thus runs
    the first line of the 114th quatrain of Heron-Allen's:
    "The world being fleeting I practise naught but
    artifice."
    And he also chafes in the chains of his sins. Following
    is the 23d quatrain of the same translation:
    "Khayyam, why mourn for thy sins?
    From grieving thus what advantage more or less dost
    thou gain?
    Mercy was never for him who sins not,
    Mercy is granted for sins; why then grieve?"

Abu'l-Ala, in a quatrain which I did not translate, goes even farther in his questioning perplexity.

"Why do good since thou art to be forgiven for thy sins?" he asks.

20. "Kaaba Stone," the sacred black stone in the Kaaba at Meccah.

21. The American poet, Lowell, in "The Crisis," utters the same cry:

> "Truth forever on the scaffold,
> Wrong forever on the throne."

22. "And the poor beetle that we tread upon
> In corporal sufferance finds a pang as great
> As when a giant dies."
> —Shakespeare: Measure for Measure.

> "To let go a flea is a more virtuous act than to give a dirham to a beggar."—Abu'l-Ala.

23. Omar too, in the 157th quatrain of Heron-Allen's—
> "Had I charge of the matter I would not have come,
> And likewise could I control my going, where could I go?"

24. "Thy two soul-devouring angels," the angels of death and resurrection.

25. "Nubakht," one of the opponents of the Prophet Mohammed.

26. "Rabbi," my lord God.

27. "And like the dead of Ind," referring to the practice of the Hindus who burn their dead.

> "Munker" and "Nakir," the two angels who on the Day of Judgment open the graves of the dead and cross-examine them—the process is said to be very cruel—as to their faith. Whosoever is found wanting in this is pushed back into the grave and thence thrown into Juhannam. No wonder Abu'l-Ala prefers cremation.

28. He wrote his own epitaph, which is:
> "This wrong to me was by my father done,
> But never by me to any one."

29. "Izrail," the angel of death.

30. These will suggest to the reader Shakespeare's lines:
> "Imperial Caesar, dead and turned to clay,

Might stop a hole to keep the wind away;
O, that that earth, which kept the world in awe,
Should stop a wall t'expel the winter's flaw."

31. Compare this with Omar's:
"Thou hast no power over the morrow,
And anxiety about the morrow is useless to thee:
Waste not thou the moment, if thy heart is not mad,
For the value of the remainder of thy life is not
certain."

www.ingramcontent.com/pod-product-compliance
Lightning Source LLC
Chambersburg PA
CBHW060501160726
47992CB00003B/1270